# DARK BODY LANGUAGE

## discover how 97% of the people out there are using body language to manipulate your mind

### Elisa Ferranti

On September 27, I managed to reach a total of 1700 people who started following my education.

Marco and I want to thank you for becoming one of us, and we have a surprise for you.

I'm writing to you to let you know that if you buy the paper version, you will have the free kindle version of this book for you and for anyone you want.

I am doing it because I want as many people as possible to approach these concepts to understand how manipulation and body language work.

So, if you know people who would be interested in the subject who are curious and eager to learn new things, don't wait to give them this book without spending a cent.

Happy reading and good handling

# INTRODUCTION

**Do you know what is the only skill that still today 97% of people don't know that makes you make the big leap in your work and social life, and anything else?**

Have you ever wondered what kind of information is available from your body, how important it is and who can read it? Did you know there is now a growing interest in profiting from learning to interpret this overlooked area of human behavior?

One of the most influential modes of conversation we make use of in our day to day interactions is our non-verbal, or body language.

It is the mode of communication which ignites our "gut level" feelings and responses. Research has proven that obtaining an understanding of body language will increase one's capability to be successful at getting anything one wants out of any given situation.

Without wasting much of your time in this book, there are several steps you can take to improve your interpretation and use of body language.

So let's get started.

# CHAPTER 1

## Knowing the body langauge

Knowing a little about body language is like learning to read between the lines.

We say things with our eyes and make different gestures with our bodies to get our point across. Simultaneously, reading someone else's body movements can fill in the blanks of a conversation for us.

Body language is an unspoken conversation that happens whenever we communicate. We use it every day, and most of us aren't even aware of it.

Not only don't we realize it in ourselves, but we also fail to understand what others are saying to us.

Body language is a compelling method of communication that you can recognize saying a word.

Body language includes many different gestures and uses all body parts, including the eyes, head, arms, hands, and legs.

Each gesture could have more than one meaning, so it is essential to keep the gesture properly when you interpret its meaning.

Being aware of the message you are sending with your own body could change your life. Once you are aware of the movements, you can become a better communicator. On a job interview, talking with friends, or looking to meet new friends, you will look at others in a brand new way when you try to read what they say with their bodies.

Our voice may be saying one thing while our body language is saying quite the opposite.

Keep in mind that when evaluating body language, it is always better to look for a combination of expressions.

If you base your evaluation of body language on just one word you see, you may be entirely wrong in your conclusion.

Someone that looks up to the left with their eyes during conversation may not be necessarily lying. The person could be thinking of a creative way to answer a question.

**Body language basics you should know:**

When someone is stroking their chin, this could mean they are making a decision on something. Some people stroke their cheek or hair when making a decision. Clasping or putting the hands together upwards as if to pray, has also been used when making a decision. When a person tilts their head, this normally means they are interested in more information. Dogs and robots do this to express they are waiting for more information. My wife and son constantly bite their nails. While this normally means a person is nervous or insecure about something, it could also mean they have a bad habit.

When you notice someone pinching their nose (without hands) and/or closing their eyes, this normally means they are reacting negatively to something.

I knew a man who would close his eyes when people would talk to him, but he did not pinch his nose. If you knew him well enough, you would know that he was just trying to tune into a spiritual vibe for direction in the conversation. I hear that when someone touches or slightly rubs their nose, they may be lying or expressing doubt about something. I do not know how true that is. Maybe they just have an itch.

Body language basic gets a bad reputation is when someone has their hands clasped behind their back. The idea here is that they are apprehensive or frustrated about something. But in reality, I think if someone is apprehensive or frustrated, they would be in a position of readiness to do something.

Instead, I believe when someone has their hands behind their backs, it would most likely mean they are relaxed.

When people leave the military, they have this habit of feeling at ease. Another basic body language that I believe is misunderstood, is when someone is standing with their hands on their hips.

This position is said to mean one is in a state of aggression. But, once again, I believe this could be simply a position of rest or confidence.

Lastly, two more body language basics exist. If you notice someone sitting down with their legs wide open, that means they are comfortable with you.

If their palms are exposed to you, that means they mean you no harm and want to connect with you. What are your basic body language expressions telling others? Many of us are really talking with our body without even knowing it.

Taking action with your body usually means that we are in control of subconscious mind and that are part of our nature. Making body language as one of our communicating languages to others, than maybe that is sometimes the best way to communicate to others.

Types of body language

There are also different types of nonverbal communication. As we learn about each type of nonverbal signal, keep in mind that nonverbals often work in concert with each other, combining to repeat, modify, or contradict the verbal message being sent.

• Facial expressions. The human face is extremely expressive, able to convey countless emotions without saying a word. And unlike some forms of nonverbal communication, facial expressions are universal. The facial expressions for happiness, sadness, anger, surprise, fear, and disgust are the same across cultures.

• Body movement and posture. Consider how your perceptions of people are affected by the way they sit, walk, stand, or hold their head. The way you move and carry yourself communicates a wealth of information to the world. This type of nonverbal communication includes your posture, bearing, stance, and the subtle movements you make.

• Gestures. Gestures are woven into the fabric of our daily lives. You may wave, point, beckon, or use your hands when arguing or speaking animatedly, often expressing yourself with gestures without thinking. However, the meaning of some gestures can be very different across cultures. While the "OK" sign made with the hand, for example, usually conveys a positive message in English-speaking countries, it's considered offensive in countries such as Germany, Russia, and Brazil. So, it's important to be careful of how you use gestures to avoid misinterpretation.

• Eye contact. Since the visual sense is dominant for most people, eye contact is an especially important type of nonverbal communication. The way you look at someone can communicate many things, including interest, affection, hostility, or attraction. Eye contact is also important in maintaining the flow of conversation and for gauging the other person's interest and response.

• Touch. We communicate a great deal through touch. Think about the very different messages given by a weak handshake, a warm bear hug, a patronizing pat on the head, or a controlling grip on the arm, for example.

• Space. Have you ever felt uncomfortable during a conversation because the other person was standing too close and invading your space? We all have a need for physical space, although that need differs depending on the culture, the situation, and the closeness of the relationship. You can use physical space to communicate many different nonverbal messages, including signals of intimacy and affection, aggression or dominance.

• Voice. It's not just what you say, it's how you say it. When you speak, other people "read" your voice in addition to listening to your words. Things they pay attention to include your timing and pace, how loud you speak, your tone and inflection, and sounds that convey understanding, such as "ahh" and "uh-huh." Think about how your tone of voice can indicate sarcasm, anger, affection, or confidence.

## The Importance of Body Language

Body language is a part of communication that very few people study. Yet, it makes up most of what we use to communicate and is generally much more accurate a judge of meaning than are the words we use. I'm going to share some reasons why body language is so important and then give you a brief quiz to take to see how well you understand its meaning.

They say actions speak louder than words, and sometimes we can communicate things even without the aid of a single word. We can shrug our shoulders and, without a word, we've just said, "I don't know." We can raise our eyebrows, and we've just said, "Excuse me? Did I hear you right?" We can turn our hands over palms up in front of us to say, "I don't know what else to say. That's all I've got." And we can point to our nose to indicate that the other person's "got it right!"

Some of the things we say with our bodies can help us reinforce why we are saying it. Simply saying "I don't know" has got nothing on adding the following gestures.

We can turn our hands over face up in front of us as we raise our eyebrows and invert our smile while we stick our bottom lip slightly out and look to the side. Now we've also made someone laugh and perhaps taken a bit of the pressure off ourselves

or the other person who was a bit nervous about not knowing whatever it was we didn't know.

Further, paying attention to someone's body language can help us discern when someone is not telling us the whole truth and nothing but the truth. Here are a few signs that someone might be lying. Often a person who is not telling the truth or all of the fact will not want to make eye contact for fear the eyes are the windows to their lying souls. However, there are also other signs of lying.

A person who isn't telling the whole truth may clear their throat, stammer or change their pitch as if to try and sway your attention away from their lie or to stall so they may have time to think up a valid answer or plausible explanation. Additionally, foot-tapping or bouncing, blushing, putting their hand to their face, turning away or raising their shoulders may be indicators that they are uncomfortable with the conversation because they are not telling the truth.

Another essential function of body language is to express our feelings about what we are discussing. Body language can help us determine how someone feels about what they are saying! For example, a person may tell her boss that she would be happy to take the account. Still, her body language might indicate that she is not pleased about it; this can be an essential tidbit that can help a manager determine who is the best person to handle this assignment. If her heart isn't in it, she may do an adequate job when another employee might turn this small job into a lifelong client.

Body language may be the determining factor in a job interview. Suppose the applicant's body language conveys that he is at ease with the subject matter and gives confidence. In that case, he has a higher probability of getting the job, especially in this tough job market.

In a friendship, one's body language can indicate that someone is paying attention or doesn't care about what the other person is saying. Leaning forward into the conversation shows that this person is interested in hearing what the other person is saying.

Leaning back would indicate that he was disinterested or felt superior. Leaning forward and standing close while talking may suggest that someone is aggressively trying to persuade the other person or trying to dominate the conversation. While not making eye contact, listening to someone indicates that you are not paying attention but are waiting for your chance to speak.

Somebody language is more obvious to discern, but other kinds of body language are not so easy. Let's see if we can try your hand. I'll give you a few questions to see how well you read body language.

1. What does it mean when someone puts their palm to their chest?

a) Superiority

b) Confidence

c) Sincerity

2. What does it mean when someone rubs their nose?

a) Superiority

b) Dislike

c) Anger

3. What message does it convey when someone looks over their glasses at someone?

a) Contempt

b) Scrutiny

c) Superiority

4. What does it convey when a person looks up and to the right before they speak?

a) They are trying to recall something

b) They are lying

c) They are trying to make something up

Answers:

1. c) Sincerity

2. b) Dislike

3. b) Scrutiny

4. a) They are trying to recall some facts (mainly for those who are right-handed)

How'd you do?

Studies show that 70% of our communication is acquired nonverbally and far more accurately than the words we use. Therefore, we must learn to use and discern body language more effectively to become effective communicators. By understanding body language more effectively, we can increase our chances of spotting a liar, maintaining our friendships, hiring, and hiring. For many more reasons, body language and communication skills, in general, will help each of us immeasurably in our professional and personal life.

# Chapter 2

# How to Read Body Language and Signs of Attraction

Our body language gives us away.

As men, we notice, but as women, they seal our fate based entirely on the way we carry ourselves and the way we hold her eyes with us when we talk or listen. It's an amazing gift they have, the ability to tell us all about ourselves just through the messages our bodies send when we sit, stand, walk, talk, or listen.

They can tell whether we have a low self image, whether we are nervous or confident.

They can even tell whether our fathers were losers bums or our mothers mistreated us. How they glean all of this information from the way we hold our bodies, I will never know. But I know that making yourself aware of your body and body language is well worth the effort.

Okay, so you have some pretty poor posture and you slouch when you sit and tend to look down (or chest level) too often. Sure, I could tell you the benefits of wandering about your home balancing a book on the top of your head, but that type of serious posturing is really more for the Baryshnikov types of the world. Men don't normally walk like that. However, check out your stance in the mirror. What is your impression of you when you see you standing there? Do your shoulders sag forward as though you're carrying some terrible family secret? Are you? Do you give yourself a double chin but slouch forward at the hips and maintain a downward glance? These things are correctable, and they are correctable in two ways.

Correcting poor body language can be done either from the outside or the inside. If you are going to correct it from the outside, you are going to have to become aware of your posture all of the time until it becomes a habit. In most cases, you have to perform a task repetitively for at least thirty days before it becomes habitual. Check out your walk, the way you sit, and the way you stand. These are the three basic body language positions that will give you away very quickly. You might be a fabulous guy with great partner potential. She'll never know that unless you stand up straighter and look at her directly, but gently, in the eyes when talking and listening. If you have a dog or a cat, practice looking at them while talking if you feel silly practicing with yourself in the mirror.

Of course, maybe you don't want to practice at all at home. It seems like a girly thing to do, doesn't it? It's your choice but relieving yourself of an old habit is almost impossible without sufficient practice. Spending a little time evaluating your posture can save you years in the dating scene. If you aren't going to practice at home, then practice absolutely everywhere you go. Stand up straighter, look everyone in the eye with a direct but kind gentleness, shake hands like a man, and walk like you have purpose.

You can also help enhance your posture by working from the inside out. Usually, it is our emotional baggage that brings our shoulders down and prevents us from making firm but gentle eye contact. It can be the gift of abuse your parents gave you or it can be some horrendous secret you feel you keep from the world, but dragging and sagging shoulders are definitely a sign of feeling afoul. Eye contact is difficult for those who haven't been able to feel good about themselves. Using eye contact can feel intimidating and even a little vulnerable. Thus, women receive a lot more information by the way your eyes react to hers than anything else. If they dart away quickly, they see deceit. If they continually cruise to her chest, she will see a pig. And if they stay cemented on the floor, she will see an emotional project.

The more you feel about yourself, the more likely you are to walk with authority, stand up straight, create warm and inviting eye contact, and of course, appear approachable even from a distance. The more you can forgive yourself for your past mistakes and the more you realize that you have immense value in this world, the more open you will appear because you will honestly become more open. Aside from the huge bonus of sending off the right physical signals to the women you hope to meet, you will also feel like a downright way better person with a lot to offer any woman. You might even be surprised at the changes that can happen in other areas of your life.

Men with strong postures are more readily promoted, have more intelligent and attractive wives, and even have more friends. Using good posture to portray that you are a strong and proud man is a normal part of our everyday living. Of course, since we've been out of high school long enough to forget the ruler up the back when we were slouching in our seats, we might need to find other ways of reminding ourselves that we need to walk tall and stand with confidence. Posturing is so vital that men have been known to take week-long seminars on improving your posture. Every one of those seminars runs about $1000 minimum, with many in the $3000 to $5000 range. It seems a little cheaper to dig deep, let go, and believe in yourself. You are a good catch. It is perfectly okay for you to know that fact.

Women know when you're faking it. They seem to have an innate radar that tells them exactly what you are feeling and how much you don't want them to know. Your eye contact will tell them everything they need and more within the first thirty seconds of meeting. No matter what your little fluff belly might look like or your concerns are regarding the size of your personal matters, your eyes are her peephole into whether she has the time to stop and talk to you or not. Given that, it would truly make sense to spend some time evaluating how much you give away with you eyes and your body's posture in order to come across as the competent and capable man you really are.

How to Understand Male Body Language and Signs of Attraction

The pose and posture, or stance, that men use when they stand can say a lot about their attitude and emotions in a particular situation or with a particular person. A normally confident man who is intimidated by another man might subconsciously take on a different stance.

A man who is typically meek might take on a dominant stance with women if they feel that they are superior. Studies have shown that the stance men take during conversations is largely a reflexive movement that does not give much thought.

However, some men have successfully learned to use this body language of men movements and consciously make use of them to emit the attitude that they hope to convey.

**Dominant Stance**

When a man stands with their shoulders squared off and hips facing forward with hands down at the sides, it is a dominant stance. This means that the man is extremely confident and feels that they are dominant over the person they are speaking with. This stance can also be used intentionally when a man wants to exert dominance over someone that they are not necessarily already dominant with.

How to read male body language and signs of attraction can be pretty easy. It is because body language is designed to be read and it is followed by his sense of attraction. Body language will reveal probably more information than speaking the words. You don't need to be a mind reader to be able to read him. All you have to do is pay attention to what he does.

## 1. Eye contact

If there are no rules in any relationship, there is however a rule in body language. To measure his interest simply count how many times you caught him staring and for how long he holds your gaze.

Obviously when a guy is interested, he wants to get your attention through visual interaction.

## 2. Body position

His body position can be interpreted in many ways. Usually when a man is interested, he will lean towards you when you are together. He also stands right next to you. If he does it this way, he wants you to be more than his friend.

## 3.                      Preening

How to read male body language and signs of attraction are basically based on how he grooms himself on the spot. Usually he straightens his shirt and his tie. He would run his fingers on his hair and brush the "dusts" on his shirt that don't exist. As he does this, notice how he smiles. He might not be aware of it but you do.

## 4. First impression

Since men know that women usually look into attitude more than the physical, they usually have the need to be polite all the time. He will always find his manners and become the gentleman that women crave.There is really no need to be concerned about how to read male body language and signs of attraction. Men can be easy to read if you just pay attention to them.

Frequently Asked Questions (FAQs)

How do you tell if a man is attracted to you?

When it comes to men and body language, there are many body language cues that let you know a man may be attracted to you. Learn how men convey messages by reading body language. It may surprise you to learn -- by reading body language cues -- that men aren't always attracted to the best-looking woman in the room.

**What body language indicates attraction?**

When a man is attracted to a woman a key body language cue to look for is in his eyes. Dilated pupils are often part of a guy's body language that tells you they may be into you. Studies show that when a man takes a look at a woman he is physically attracted to his pupils will dilate in response. This is one of the many body language secrets many people aren't aware of.

**What does it mean when a guy is touchy with you?** An obvious clue to male attraction is a guy becoming "touchy and feely." Men are more attracted to a woman they feel relaxed with. Touching is a body language that men use to see if a woman is available to date or get to know better. Men like availability to be clear, so they may touch you as a gesture of interest. By becoming good at reading body language, you'll learn to understand the difference between aggressive touching and flirting. Always keep in mind aggressive or unwanted touching -- is never okay.

**What are the signs of attraction?**

Women often spend time evaluating others, whereas men and body appearance are often the most important factors. Men often use body language clues to determine whether a woman is interested. Whereas a woman who engages in conversation with a man will often use verbal cues to decipher interest.

**How can you tell if someone finds you attractive?**

Studies show that men find women attractive who possess the specific qualities they seek in a mate. This is the same for women. While some people are comfortable talking verbally about their attraction, others feel more comfortable reading body language before revealing their true emotions.

**How do you know if a guy finds you attractive body language?**

When you begin paying close attention to body language cues and training the brain to read body language, you'll find that the majority of women (and men) are naturally good at reading each other's body language clues. Wondering what body language cue do men notice first? Studies show that men find direct expressions of affection and small gestures like hair tossing easy to interpret.

**How do you know if a man is hiding his feelings?**

Many people believe that men and women lie differently. When it comes to male body language or men and women lying and hiding feelings, male body language and female body language can be very similar. Signs of men, women, lying often include averted eyes and avoiding eye contact when being dishonest or withholding the truth.

**What do guys touches mean?**

When it comes to male body language -- the majority of women automatically assume that when a guy touches you it means he's attracted to you. While touching can indicate that a guy is attracted to you, men use different areas of the body to convey attraction.

For example, if a man is interested in a woman he may hold her gently around the waist. (A man that is holding a woman high above the waist and around the shoulders is more likely conveying friendly affection than attraction.)

## Do shy guys initiate conversation?

If you're wondering what cue do men find easiest to pick up on, it's a conversation. Shy guys can easily pick up on verbal cues from a woman they are attracted to. If they are genuinely attracted, they may initiate a conversation.

## What does eye contact mean to a guy?

Lingering eye contact with a guy can indicate interest or attraction. If your eyes happen to fall in the vicinity of your favorite male body part, a guy will often interpret this as sexual interest. When someone is interested in you, they may admire you from head to toe. The longer the look, the deeper the interest is likely to be.

## How to Understand Female Body Language and Signs of Attraction

### 1. The Eyes.

If her eyes are dilated or widely opened, that means she's interested or may even be sexually attracted to you. Here's another way to find out if she likes you. Notice if she looks at you longer-than-usual, glances her eyes away for a while (she may look down or on her sides), and then looks at you again. If she does this repeatedly (especially with a smile on her face), then she's very attracted to you.

When a woman is excited to see you, you might also notice her eyebrows rise unconsciously.

## 2.                        The                        Lips.

You'll know if a woman fancies you by reading her lips. Some female body language signals that indicate attraction include wetting                        or massaging her lips with her tongue, softly biting them, and putting on lipstick.

**3.**          **Exposing**          **their**          **neck.**
Because the neck contains the jugular vein, it's a vulnerable part of the body. In an attempt to protect themselves, a person may be inclined to reach for their neck in discomfort. When they're feeling comfortable and safe though, they might expose their necks. To do this, they could brush their hair to the side or tilt one shoulder forward and down, body language expert Blanca Cobb,          M.S.,          tells          mbg.

**4.**          **Playing**          **with**          **jewelry.**
While grabbing for the neck is generally a sign of discomfort, if a woman reaches for her necklace, she may be sending the opposite signal. If the movement is slower, sensual, and more of a caress, Cobb says that can be a sign of flirting. Fidgeting with rings, however, could be a sign of discomfort and nervousness.

**5.**          **The**          **Legs.**
If she consistently crosses and uncrosses her legs, then this is a clue that she likes you. If she's massaging and exposing her thighs while travelling and uncrossing, then this is an obvious sign of attraction.

However, if she crosses her legs tightly, she might be indicating defensiveness for a long time. She may be signalling that she's "closed" from any potential sexual encounters.

**6.** **Moving objects.**

When eating at a restaurant or sitting across from someone, a woman might move objects out of the way. This could be a sign she wants to be closer to the other person, Oud explains, particularly if it's followed by physical touch. This tends to be a sign of affection among all genders.

**6.** **The Knees.**

You can tell if a girl's interested in you by looking at her knees. If they're facing you, then that's a good sign of attraction. If she turns her other body parts towards you as if she wants to focus her attention solely on you, then you just hit the jackpot. If her knees are pointingin other directions other than yours indicate her disinterest; hence, she wants to get out of the current situation. Reading this female body language signal is vital, so you won't keep pursuing her if she's not interested anymore.

**7.                           The                           Hands.**

If a woman touches you, then this is a very reliable sign of attraction. Note that she may not feel you in an obvious manner. She may touch your arm to prove a point or come up with reasons to dust your shirt. But you know better! Isn't it fascinating how you can decode what a woman is feeling or thinking by simply reading female body language signals? Now you can do away with the guessing game and start focusing on your                           romantic                           adventures.

**8.          Showing          facial          expressions.**

The feedback loop in conversation tends to be more visible in women than men. Nodding of the head, arching the eyebrows, smiling, or saying things like 'oh, really?' may be signs of flirtation or interest, Oud explains. While men do this too, women may be generally more obvious in their flirty facial expressions.

**9.                     Playing                     with                     hair.**

When a woman plays with or twirls her hair around her finger, that can be a sign of flirtation, especially when showing the inside of          her          wrist.

According to Cobb, women will generally pull a strand from the back or side of their head when flirting. "When they're readjusting with the front, like a bang, that's more nervousness," she explains.

**10.          Turning          their          palms          upward.**

While clenched hands can be a sign of withdrawal or discomfort, open hands with palms facing upward can signal trust and openness.

**11.     Biting     or     licking     the     lips.** Biting the lip can be a sign of nervousness and flirtation— sometimes both at the same time, Cobb explains. "Some women might lick their lips," she adds. In some cases, this is done to draw attention to the lips or to moisten them before kissing.

**12.     Tilting     their     head.** "The more interested you are in somebody, the more attention you're going to give them," Cobb says. One way to show that attention is by tilting the head as someone talks or nodding for them to continue. On a more sensual note, a woman might tilt her chin down slightly, then slowly look up. "Particularly when you have the smolder look with it, that can be very captivating," she                                           says.

*"If you're a guy and you're looking for a date, you'll look to see how a woman is acting toward you. That's very fair," Cobb says. Still, avoid making assumptions and always keep the context in mind. "Just because someone smiles at you doesn't necessarily mean they like you," she adds. Instead of taking one body language cue as a sign that someone's interested, you should look for a cluster of clues that happen around the same time.*

*Even if some women demonstrate flirting in a specific way, there are always outliers, Cobb adds. When we stop taking into account people's unique tendencies, that's where stereotypes come into play.*

*Gender aside, Oud recommends anyone thinking about what their body language might be conveying to consider: Who am I, what are my behaviors and nonverbal communications, and is that effective for what I want to achieve?*

# Chapter 3

# Have Confident Body Language

Actions, like those made by one with confident body language, speak louder than words. And when people say "action", they mean more than just hand gestures or nodding of heads or showing a facial expression.

When people say "action speaks louder than words", it often means communicating through one's whole body. It's widely accepted that 93% of what we communicate is of the non-verbal kind. This being so, our body language is very important in how we come across to others.

The body can send messages that are clearer than what comes out of one's mouth, whether or not the person is aware of it. So if a person is feeling nervous or insecure, their body language will show it. They will not have the power of body language.
By the same token, when one is secure about himself, his confidence would also naturally show it.

## THE NEED FOR CONFIDENT BODY LANGUAGE
Between an insecure body language and a confident one, the latter is of course the more beneficial.

When a person feels confident, it also appears that they ARE confident. And when it does, it gives them some kind of aura that commands respect and attention from the others.

This kind of confidence can also be helpful for someone trying to land a job or getting a client to invest into their business.

No one wants to hire, let alone trust, a person who does not feel confident about themselves.

Lack of confidence means lack of skills, talent and capabilities. This is something one should avoid sending to others about themselves. So now that it is established that confident body language gestures are far better than insecure kinds, the question now comes to, how exactly does one do that?

Below are some practical tips on how to have confident body language.

## 1. LOOKS AND COMFORT

No matter what a person does to have a confident look, it would be impossible to look such if he does not feel good at all.

The first step to looking confident is feeling confident. The least thing that one can do to have such feeling is to make sure they are well-groomed, i.e., showered, with clean and neat clothing, teeth brushed, hair combed, etc. Looking and feeling good is the first step to having the confidence one needs.

## 2. TIGHTEN THAT GRIP

As mentioned above, when trying to get a job or getting a client to invest in one's business, it is imperative to show confident indications of body language. And one way to do this is to give a firm and sincere hand shake. It is wrong to show hesitation when grabbing someone's hand for a shake. What one should do is to extend their hand with confidence and shake the other's with a firm grip.

## 3. SMILE BUT DON'T FAKE IT

A confident body language also shows that a person feels good about himself.

This means that he is happy about things around him, thus he is a good source of positive energy. Let that confidence exude from within through a real and beautiful smile.

THE NO GO'S FOR YOUR ARMS AND HANDS
There are two things that a person should never, in his entire socializing life, do.

These two things are crossing one's arms and the other is putting one's hands inside the pocket.

The former shows cockiness, the latter shows boredom and indifference.

*Your body language conveys so much about what kind of person you are. It is a sure-fire way to communicate confidence, and belief you have in yourself.*

*Start applying these practical but simple confident body language tips today and soon you will exude more positivity and assuredness with all people and situations you come across.*

*Confidence is a vital quality to have. It is the springboard to you attaining more success, hapiness and fulfillment. Being confident starts with looking confident.*

## Body Language to Power Up the Message of Your Presentation

In any speech or presentation, your body language adds power to the message. It support what your words are saying. The operative word here is, of course, "support". Body language must be in tune with the message.

And the corollary is that body language must also not distract or detract from the message. If they are denying each other, then your presentation will fail.

Confidence and sincerity are the absolute basis for this process. If your body is declaring that you are not sincere in what you are saying then your credibility decreases and there is no way your message will have the impact it should have.

Think about the tone of your message. Is it relaxed, conversational? Then make your body language relaxed.

Is it passionate, strong and powerful, then create body language that conveys that power. Is it alert and enthusiastic, then your body language will be upright and reflecting that enthusiasm. You also need to be aware that your gestures can support or detract from your message. Learn to become aware of what your hands are doing while you speak. If necessary, make yourself hold them still. Many people have habits that are terribly distracting and yet they aren't aware of what they are doing. They click or twiddle a pen, play with their hair or their clothes, hold a microphone with fingers unconsciously making a rude gesture, take glasses on and off, put hands in pockets and take them out. All of these things are not necessarily detrimental in themselves, if the audience is absolutely focused on the speaker and the message. But if there is any reason for the audience's attention to stray (and we all have short attention spans) then they will become fascinated, at best, and possibly annoyed at whatever it is that the speaker is doing with their hands. If, on the other hand, (my pun!!), those hands are working to support the speech, they will bring the attention back to the message. They will also give power to the impact of the message.

**Natural gestures are basically the aim.** If you are not a natural gesturer, your body will support your message. It is necessary to be aware that you are not repeating the same gesture many times. It may add emphasis the first time, but after that it will distract as much as the others mentioned earlier. Watch television journalists and sooner or later you will notice this.

You can also practice gestures. Join a public speaking club (and I recommend ITC), where you can practise in a supportive environment until you are comfortable, and confident that your gestures are not detracting from your message.

Of course, there are many books and websites with information about body language and gestures. Basically:

Gestures above shoulder level support messages about things that are spiritual or uplifting (a church minister will raise his hands in blessing).

Ordinary messages are supported by gestures at the middle level of your body.

Things that are despicable or degrading or debilitating are supported by gestures below the waist.

You can use your palms. Held out, palm upwards, they support supplication, requesting a response, or openness. They can be used to indicate division if held vertically with the little finger down. Using a fist is a very powerful gesture. It indicates strong power and passion, and may also be used as a threat. Be careful with that. Take care, too, with pointing with a finger. People don't respond well to accusation or to being singled out, so be sure your gesture supports your message.

Your clothes, too, can distract attention from your message.

If you have a very bright or unusual item of clothing, if your scarf or tie flaps in a breeze, if your earrings dangle or click, or your necklace or tie pin clicks on a microphone, the audience will be distracted from your message.

Again, unless your message is absolutely riveting, your clothes will become the centre of attention just as gestures can, and your message will lose its impact.

How you stand and walk works in just the same way. If you are a passionate speaker who simply cannot stand still, then hopefully you will support the passion of your message. Try to use standing still to give the same sort of impact that a pause in the middle of rapid speech would give.

If you choose to move or change position just to provide relief because you think your speech is boring; be careful. It may be that your movement will have more impact than your massage. Timing can help so that you change position with a new idea or with a new visual support.

Try to make all of your body language work with the movement. So, for example, if you want to walk to give the impression of thinking of a new idea, then set your hand up to your face to indicate thoughtfulness, and speak slowly or stop speaking altogether.

Facial expression, too, must be in harmony with your message, or it will work against it, just as your body language does.

Everything - body language, image and message must work together to create the impact you have chosen.

# Chapter 4

# Does body language really matter?

There are two good reasons to master the mysteries of body language. The first is that you can control the impression that you make on others, and the second is that you can consciously become aware of what other people are thinking — sometimes before they themselves are aware of it. Becoming better at both these endeavors will serve you well in business and in life.

Most of the myths and misconceptions come from the 20th-century approach to understanding non-verbal behavior, which focuses on those few gestures in every culture that have a specific, coded meaning. Holding up two fingers as a "peace" sign, for example, or making a circle of the thumb and forefinger to say "OK" in some Western cultures.

Researchers paid little attention to the unspecific hand-waving that accompanies speech because they thought it didn't mean much in this coded kind of way. The result was that communications researchers and pop culture went on a hunt to decode as many gestures as possible in literal, one-of-a-kind terms.

Most of these so-called secrets of body language came about because of this misguided sense that gesture was a precisely meaningful result of some thought or expression. But body language doesn't work like that, and recent brain research has made it possible to understand much more clearly how it works and what it does mean.

The bad news is that all that vague hand-waving that accompanies speech is where the real action is. So rather than looking for specific gestures to decode (or to intimidate our colleagues with), we should rather be working to understand what the general import is of our body language and the body language of the people around us.

Here's how it works. We get an emotion, or an intent, in the unconscious part of our brain. That intent or emotion is expressed first in gesture. Only nanoseconds later does the emotion or intent reach our conscious minds. We literally gesture how we're feeling before we think (consciously) about it.

And that's the good news. By mastering your own body language, you can appeal to other people's unconscious minds, bypassing their conscious thought — or at least arriving unconscious before they realize it. By learning to read other people's body language, you can know what they're feeling or intending before they do. You can see a decision, for example, show up in body language before it arrives in the conscious mind of the person who's waving her hands. Because body language comes from emotion and intent, it tends to be fairly simple and mostly concerned with the kinds of things that matter in an evolutionary sense. Hunger, fear, trust, attraction, liking, disliking, anger, joy — these are the sorts of messages that body language reliably conveys.

Most of us are experts at reading these unconscious messages from people that we know well — family, close friends, co-workers we've known a long time. The more difficult read is of people we don't know as well. But it is incredibly helpful to know what their basic orientation is when we meet them, or when we try to close a sale, or when we're recruiting them.

In the same way, if we can master our basic emotions, like fear in a public speaking situation for example, then we can show up with confident body language that will ensure that we speak with impact.


Basic things to look for when you're first meeting someone

Are they open to you, or closed? Are they friends or foes? Look to see how much they're doing to protect themselves (closed) by putting their hands in front of their stomachs, for example. How close do they come to you? Do they stay close after shaking your hand, or do they draw away? We move closer to people we trust, and away from people that we don't trust. And we humans are very adept at measuring small changes in body and head positions that indicate those emotions.

Instead of trying to decode (or impose) specific gestures, look for the general orientation, and for some basic issues. What matters to you in a particular situation will guide you in what to look for. If you're trying to win over a customer, look for signs of agreement and trust (head nodding, closeness). If you're trying to recruit an employee, look for signs of alignment (mirroring). Body language is very basic, and very simple, but that doesn't mean that it can't convey powerful messages.

## How can your body language improve your mood?

Our body language is the way that we connect not only with our external world, but it is also a way that we connect with ourselves. How do you treat yourself? Do you hunch over when you walk or do you walk tall and fulfilled? Are you are grateful for every single movement that your body makes for you?

Probably not; we often take our body for granted, we often choose to criticise it. Body language can not only influence our physical body and posture, but it can also influence how we are feeling. Having good posture has positive effects on depression, and helps us maintain higher levels of self-esteem and positivity when we are faced with stress.

An upcoming field of psychology, known as embedded cognition, claims that the connection between our body and the world around us don't just influence us but are intimately woven into the way that we think. Studies in this field show that those sitting in a hard chair are less likely to compromise than those sitting in a soft chair, and those holding warm drinks found others to be more caring and generous than those holding cold drinks. This research indicates that body language is a two-way street leading to both the external and internal world.

# Chapter 5

# Body language in the workplace

Body language can communicate a variety of messages in the workplace. You use body language as both your private and public communication. Every time you have a conversation with a coworker, present in a meeting or introduce yourself to a customer, you are almost certainly using some kind of body language.

Body language can communicate several important messages during a workday. Importantly, body language conveys someone's level of interest or focus. If someone makes eye contact with you, nods when you speak or leans toward you while you are talking, you likely have their full attention. If someone is leaning back in their chair, constantly looking away from you or fidgeting their fingers, they might be bored or distracted. Observing and interpreting these messages is beneficial if you need to gauge how an individual or a team responds to your ideas or suggestions.

Understanding body language in the workplace can affect the entire team's productivity and relationships. If you can interpret body language accurately, you increase your skills as a professional communicator. While you work to improve your understanding of body language in the workplace, it is important to consider some key facts about body language.

First, context is a crucial part of interpreting body language. Certain actions can mean very different things depending on the person and

the situation. Crossed arms can be a sign of frustration or discomfort. However, for some, they can also show confidence or a casual attitude. The more familiar you are with your employers, coworkers or clients, the more easily you will read their unique body language.

One benefit of understanding body language in the workplace is your ability to interpret messages that are not communicated out loud. Non-verbal messages can reinforce or contradict the words someone says. A coworker might say "I agree with you completely" while subtly shaking their head. A client might say "I am really not interested" while leaning forward in their chair. These mixed messages are sometimes inconsequential, but they also have the attentional to give you some valuable insight into what another person is thinking.

Body Language Mistakes You're Making at Work A substantial portion of our communication is done through non-verbal behavior and micro expressions—subtleties that we notice and evaluate in our subconscious. In fact, only a small percentage of the brain processes verbal communication. In an age where in-person communication is becoming less common, body language is more important than ever. It can help you exude confidence, trustworthiness, and build relationships at work. Whether you want to land a promotion, ace a presentation, or nail a job interview, it's essential to master the unspoken dynamics at play. Avoid these common body language pitfalls to be more confident and successful at work:

## 1. Mind is not attuned to the body

When our mind is not in congruence with our body, we may try to portray a state which is in conflict with our inner self by controlling our posture and expression on our face, but sooner or later this incongruence will show up in our body language.

A positive body language cannot keep up with the negative mental state – what goes up in our mind will show up in our body. Without our realisation, these "microexpressions" will be noticeable to the people around us.

"Our body language expresses our mental state whether we like it or not. Our facial expressions, voice posture, and all the other components of body language reflect our mental and emotional condition every second. Because we don't control this flow consciously, whatever is in our head will show up in our body language", says Olivia Fox Cabane.

How to align our mind and the body

Research shows that our mind cannot distinguish imagination from reality. So, whatever our mind believes, our body will project.

We can bring out the desired body language by catching ourselves in those moments of negative mental states – disagreement, insecurity, angst, frustration, anxiety, criticism and self-doubt, and choosing to get into a positive one.

When you need to project confidence, seek inspiration

When you feel angst due to a disagreement, ask yourself "What can I learn from the other person" and "How are my biases causing me to be closed-minded"

When all you can see is negativity, choose to ask "What's the one positive thing I can think about this situation"

When self-doubt consumes you, tell yourself "I need to let go of my fears to create a better version of myself"

When you exaggerate a negative outcome, ask yourself "what's the worst that can happen" and "Is it really that bad or am I making up stories"

Adopting a positive frame of reference and moving from a problem to a solution mindset can help us shift gears from a negative internal state to a positive one.

## We do not make a commitment to be present

"Being present—paying attention to what's going on rather than being caught up in your thoughts—can yield immense rewards. When you exhibit presence, those around you feel listened to, respected, and valued", explains Olivia Fox Cabane.

When we are not engaged in a conversation, consumed in our own thoughts and pretend to listen, it clearly shows up in the non-verbal signals we send to the other person.
We may start fidgeting with our phone or laptop showing signs of distraction, look here and there instead of making eye contact signaling we are not interested in what they have to say and may even shift too many times in our position out of discomfort.

Without our awareness, our body language will convey disrespect and distrust to the other person.

How to be present

"You must commit to a conversation, even the brief ones, or walk away. If you're too distracted, admit that to both yourself and the other person. Be present or be gone", Celeste Headlee advises in We Need to Talk.

It's more polite to walk away from the conversation that doesn't interest you than pretend to be present.
Once you decide to participate, you first need to convince and tell yourself that you want to be present.

Say "I choose to be present" and then adopt body language that aligns with it – look at the other person with enthusiasm, lean just a little to build interest and try to grasp what the other person intends to say.

May occasionally drift away, but by choosing to be mentally present, you can bring your mind back to the conversation. Active listening though difficult is the most effective form of non-verbal communication that requires continuous practice and training of the mind.

## We ignore context

When we talk to someone, their perception of us is based on the context of the meeting, their expectations and their own personal and cultural filters.

Without recognising that people operate within a certain context, we may send non-verbal signals that conflict with their values, contradicts with their mental state or even violates their sense of self.

How to apply context

When engaged in a difficult conversation, without empathising with how the other person might be feeling in the moment, we may appear cold, unemotional and downright rude. By adopting kindness and warmth in our body language, we can convey the right message without necessarily making them feel bad someone is passed up for a promotion, showing an attitude of indifference without understanding the value it holds in their life can make them resent you. Body language that shows presence and concern by giving them an opportunity to express their feelings can build better relationships.

When a co-worker is grieving a personal loss, you may appear too intrusive in your body language when all they need is space to let the feelings subside. It could be a personal preference or a cultural nuance, but without understanding their context you may actually do more harm than good.

When dealing with difficult people, your body language may switch to a fight-or-flight response. But, if you take a moment to analyse the situation without being at the effect of fundamental attribution error, you may understand the rationale behind their behaviour.

Every situation is unique. We need to project the right body language for each person by taking their context and personal filters into account.

## We tell a conflicting story

We may believe that we are highly approachable, but others may find us unapproachable. We may also think that we are open-minded, while others may find us biased. We may assume that we provide a psychologically safe environment to our people, but our employees may be terrified to make mistakes. Now, it's easy to say that "it's just them, not me. I have already communicated to them multiple times". But really, is that the true story. Your intention may be far from the reality of your situation.

"Just after we observe what others do and just before we feel some emotion about it, we tell ourselves a story. We add meaning to the action we observed. We make a guess at the motive driving the behavior. Why were they doing that? We also add judgment— is that good or bad? And then, based on these thoughts or stories, our body responds with an emotion", says Kerry Patterson in Crucial Conversations.

When our body language doesn't match our words, people pick up on our non-verbal signals – the sign of contempt on our face when someone makes a mistake, pacing back and forth when conveying bad news, showing nervousness by fidgeting when asking for feedback, rolling eyes when we disagree, making hand gestures that signal blame and so on.

So, while you may communicate one thing with your words, your body may speak the opposite. And when people get confusing signals, they tend to go with what they observed and not what they heard.

### How to tell the right story

Bring your body language in sync with the message you wish to convey. People find it easy to trust a person when their body language reflects their words.

When asking for feedback, look the person in the eye and don't be distracted. When someone makes a mistake, show curiosity in your face to enable them to learn from their mistakes. When telling people to feel comfortable to approach you, make the open arm hand gestures. When communicating bad news, be intense but show confidence in your ability to make things right by looking at people with passion and hope.

People spend a lot of time perfecting their speech without verifying what their speech is conveying through their body. When it comes to making the right impression, don't just speak through your words, make your body language count too.

## 5. Nervous gestures

Leg jiggling, hair twirling, face touching—any other motion you do when nervous or bored—indicates insecurity. If you're prone to hand movements, find a place for them such as on a table or your hips to rest instead.

# 6.  Poor  eye  contact

A good formula for maintaining eye contact that's confident and certain (read: not creepy) is to shoot for holding a person's gaze for 50-60% of the time you're interacting with him or her. Think about the last conversation you had: Can you remember the color of the person's eyes? If not, it's probably a sign that the eye contact wasn't sufficient. Play a game with yourself and set a goal of noticing this the next time you're speaking with someone face-to-face. If you can master this, chances are others will perceive you as engaged.

**7.**       **Facing**       **away**       **from**       **people**

Check to make sure that you're not angled toward the door when engaged in conversation with people, which shows disinterest and distraction.

Instead subtly mirror or mimic their gestures. Why? When we have rapport with someone we're interacting with, we tend to angle our bodies toward them and subtly match their movements. For example, without being too obvious, place your hands on the table if theirs are, or lean slightly back in your chair if they are doing the same. This expresses harmony andalignment.

## 8.CrossedArms

Crossing your arms, which many of us do out of habit, can indicate defensiveness and self-protection. Instead, try to adopt an open stance with your arms by your side, slightly out from your body. This shows openness and confidence. Try holding something such as a notebook during important face-to-face conversations to keep your hands occupied.

## 9.Smallness

When we're feeling intimidated or uncertain, we tend to "shrink" ourselves, slouching and hunching our shoulders. This may communicate fear, powerlessness, or even laziness and lack of motivation (which obviously is the opposite effect you're going for!)

The next time you notice yourself becoming small in a meeting or tough conversation, sit up straight. Relax your shoulders back and down. Lean slightly forward. Not only will this make you appear more assured in high-pressure situations, but you'll also begin to feel that way, too. Body language can have a subtle, but powerful, psychological effect on how you're perceived at work. More importantly, research shows adopting certain body language boosts self-esteem. By avoiding these common body language mistakes, you'll not only feel more confident and self-assured, you'll become more successful in the process. This post previously appeared on Fairygodboss, which helps women get the inside scoop on pay, corporate culture, benefits, and work flexibility. Founded in 2015, Fairygodboss offers company ratings, job listings, discussion boards, and career advice.

**Body language tips for your next interview**

- Breathe calmly and deeply prior to the interview in order to relax and supply more oxygen to the brain.
- Practice a relaxed and sincere smile.
- Make sure you maintain regular eye contact.
- Maintain an open posture, do not cross your arms.
- Be engaged – nod and smile when appropriate.

- Practice your handshake, it should be firm but not too hard.
- Dress for the part – you must convey professionalism and dress for the job you want, not the job you have.

# 1 HOW YOUR MIND WORKS

**In this module, you will understand how your mind works.**

It is a fundamental part of understanding how to do mental manipulation of people. But if you don't know how the mind works, how can you make these changes?

Easy, you cannot. So I'll give you a friend's advice. Read this chapter at least three times before moving on with the book. You will understand the reason why I ask you to do so afterward!

**INTERESTING FACTS**

Now I will list you several interesting facts about the mind that you surely do not know.

The unconscious mind is re-programmed in three ways:

- Shock or dramatic event
- Repetition
- Hypnosis

In the first case, we have that situation in which, for example, you can find a boy whose father has died for any cause.

How many guys do you know who, after a misfortune, put their heads in place and maybe stopped spending money on nonsense and changed their lifestyle? We hear a lot of these cases.

**But why did this happen?**

At the exact moment when a person is overwhelmed by bad or good news for him, millions of emotions are evoked in the human mind, ready to change a part of the person's brain.

In the second case, we find repetition.

It is the model that matters most to me because it is what I always use and what works best. Look at advertising, for example.

That works when you do not notice it.

Maybe you are cleaning the house, and if the TV is on, you can hear in the background advertising. You cannot resist that force if you listen to it, and the next time you walk out of a supermarket, you'll have a cart full of products you know the slogan by heart.

You know them not because you thought: "let me hear what this advertisement says".

It does not happen, but it works to condition you just because you hear it. Try to make up your mind and think of all the advertising slogans that come to mind.

They are at least 5. You bought these products, didn't you? The answer is yes.

In the third case, we find hypnosis instead. It is the least probable condition that can happen.

To start with hypnosis, you have to study a lot, and above all, you have to find a person who wants to undergo hypnosis.

Previously, we saw how ads manipulate you. Well, through hypnosis it is not possible.

The other person must want to be hypnotized, or at least they have to be someone you have a lot of control over, and this is far more difficult. Now I'm going to talk to you about another fundamental thing to understand before we start talking about real manipulation.

Our mind works in pictures.

The mind does not think by means of letters but are the images that create the sensations. I'll give you an example.

Think of a dog. You are not thinking about the word d-o-g but you are thinking of an image of a dog, it is bringing you positive or negative emotions.

**Or maybe if I told you what color your wardrobe is?**

**How many doors does it have?**

**Which side does it open on? Left to right or the other way around?**

You are now seeing yourself in front of your wardrobe. It is not possible to answer the questions I asked you BY HEART. This is a powerful weapon to use during manipulation because you will be able to create feelings and emotions in the person who will then follow you in what you tell him to do.

## CONSCIOUS MIND AND SUBCONSCIOUS

Our mind consists of two large parts. The conscious and subconscious mind. The difference between the two is very important to understand if you want to manipulate people.

The conscious mind represents all those thoughts that we strive to do. I can give you an example of you. How many times have you said, "No, I don't have to eat this sandwich because it's not healthy", but then you ate it anyway?

I guess many times.

We have to work on people's unconscious. That is what they think. Otherwise, we won't see any lasting changes over time.

Think for example about the first time you drove.
You had to work hard to think where to put your feet and how to change the gears, press this turn up that.

That is a conscious effort. You had to think about it.

Now you drive by talking on the phone or thinking about something else. But if you are distracted, who is driving? Your unconscious mind that now understands the mechanisms and goes by itself. This is what we have to do when handling.

We need to make sure to change the behaviors and thoughts that people have.

Now, let's get to the heart of the book. But without this part on the mind, nothing would have made logical sense, and it would have been useless.

**REMEMBER TO READ THIS CHAPTER MULTIPLE TIMES.**

This way you get into the repetition case. As I told you, by repetition, this information will enter your subconscious and you will know it for the rest of your life.

Otherwise, in a few days, you will forget everything and go back to your former status.

# 2 THE DARK TRIAD

The Dark Triad is the set of different pathologies so-called "dark" that makes the person who is affected by it to have bad intentions.

The three personalities that are part of the Dark Triad are:

- Narcissism
- Machiavellianism
- Psychopathy

When a person is in the Dark Triad, it does not mean that he necessarily has all of these pathologies.

But he has just hints of them all.

Generally, these people's character is precisely related to these three pathologies.

The hard part for people to understand is that in most cases, these people are thought to be attractive or successful.

But why does this happen?

The people who are inside this Dark Triad know how to accurately take only the attractive aspects of the psychic diseases that you have read above.

It means that many people remain fascinated by it.

But let's go more specifically to talk about these pathologies.

# 3 NARCISSISM

Narcissism has been known for many years, and its essence originates in ancient Greece. The story behind the birth of this pathology is as follows.

A boy named Narciso, one day looked at himself in a lake and fell in love with his reflection.

The story is very fascinating and if you happen to leap on the internet, I suggest you to read it. Now we don't need the whole story but we just have to understand what it is it.

However, this disease has not always been studied by psychology.

The first to operate in this field and to bring this disease to light was Sigmund Freud.

Even today it is described in the most famous books of psychology as a personality disorder.

In psychology, narcissism is defined as an overly important sense of self-giving and an excessive need for attention.

This leads to the narcissistic person being seen as a great person and often with a huge ego.

But, eventually, we often see him looking for attention otherwise his ego tends to go down.

A very important factor for narcissus is criticism.

They don't take this type of attack on their person well and often tend to pay attention to judgments more from others.

This of course worsens all areas of the person's life ranging from relationships to work.

Those who are part of the Dark Triad have endless problems with relationships.

It is because they always have relationships with underlying empathy problems.

Often, these people want to be in the center of attention even with their partner by constantly asking for opinions on whatever is on their mind.

I don't know if you've ever had such a relationship. It is possible since we are attracted to these people anyway.

But it happened to me, and I tell you that it is by no means a simple situation.

Also because then 99% of you are not reciprocated.

I was 25 when it happened and I carried on the relationship for two years. Then, it fell apart.

Furthermore, narcissus can see recognition as a kind of right.

But, in most cases, without any good reason to justify these request behaviors.

Another fundamental element of narcissistic people is the criticism of others.

It is upsetting thinking about how much narcissists can criticize anyone who passes in front of them. It doesn't matter if they are co-workers or perhaps a family member.

They do it, no matter what. They talk about everyone.

But why do they do it?

Always for the same reason. Narcissists MUST be the best and feel at the center of the scene.

As actors in movies, they are the protagonists, and other people spin around them.

It does not mean that those with self-esteem are narcissistic. Pay attention to these differences.

Self-esteem is different, and it is crucial to have it in our life if we don't want to be defeated by all the things that can happen.

Narcissists are capable of manipulating persons who idealize them as someone he is not.

The narcissist has endless problems in getting along with people, and often, this person destroys the life of all the others to put feel above them.

# 4 MACHIAVELLISM

The name of this attitude derives from the Italian poet Niccolò Machiavelli who lived from 1469 until 1527.

Nowadays, this philosophy is used to describe people who have strong political or professional ambitions.

If we go more specifically into psychology, Machiavellianism is used through a scale that indicates how much the person is willing to manipulate others to get the result he wants.

The Italian poet wrote The Prince.

That is nothing more than a political treatise where he expressed the concept I expressed to you earlier.

He said that in politics good intentions, charity, and sincerity were certainly important qualities that a person must have.
But, if for any reason, it would not have been possible to arrive at the result with those qualities, then deceptions and lies were also fine.

He wrote that committing to find a shortcut or fooling someone was right if that was the only way to get the results desired.

All this chaos that Machiavelli has created to date has been summed up into the phrase "the end justifies the means".

But we have interpreted it a bit as it suited us.

The poet has not written anywhere to cheat at all costs as long as we get to the point we want.

He first looks for all the possible "soft" solutions or the legitimate ones and if he fails, then he makes use of the "hard" ones.

Nowadays, we tend to forget the real intentions of Machiavelli, and instead, we acclimate his strategies to our purposes, without thinking about the consequences.

Look at politics. They don't even try to get things done right without manipulation or the usage of tricks.
Just look at the last American elections to understand where we have come and how much we do not follow this principle.

Machiavellianism is indeed highly present in politics today.

To enter this aspect, a threat from you who are higher up is enough to make me do things in your favor simply because otherwise, I end badly.

This is a very strong symbol of Machiavellianism.

To date, many people overlook the fact that Machiavellism exists and thus approve without even knowing it the behavior of the political class and the attitudes of large companies.

The fact is that, due to the Dark Triad, these entities are taking more and more decision-making power over the fate of the world, while the population weakens more and more.

Machiavellian people are all those people who decide whether to use a cold approach or a manipulative one.

It is not all those people who harm regardless.

People with the machiavellian behavior, think thoroughly about the possibility to use a harmless way to do things, and, just after this investigation, they decide how to act.

I'll give you an example.

Surely, it will have happened to you one day not to go to school or work by claiming "I'm sick" while maybe it wasn't true.

No worries, it is common to do it once in a lifetime.

However, most people feel guilty after taking this action.

We feel like horrible people.

The Machiavellian person may not feel guilty. Just because he wanted to reach a goal, and that was the only way to do it, and maybe he does it again and again.

If they see lies and lies as the only way out, they will use them without problems.

# 5 PSYCHOPATHY

Today, psychopathy is defined as a mental disorder that has several specific characteristics

Some of these are:
- anti-social behavior
- zero empathy
- amorality
- egocentrism
- zero personal relationships
- inability to learn from past actions

The most visible of all these characteristics is antisocial behavior.

Who suffers from this disturb is lead to not follow the rules.

It does not matter if this behavior is for criminal activity or personal protest, these people do not understand that they are wrong.

Another critical characteristic that people suffering from this pathology have is amorality.

On this point, we need to pause for a moment and understand well what we are talking about.

Many people confuse amorality with immorality.

But these are two completely different things. If a person is immoral, he will still be able to understand if something is wrong or not.

For example, if you are stopped by the police because of speeding, you know you were wrong and you recognize it.

While, if the same situation happens to an amoral person, he will not be able to recognize the mistake he has just made, and indeed he will get angry with others.
So amorality is in effect a psychic pathology.

The not very positive, actually pretty scary fact, is that all people affected by this pathology tend to worsen over time.

They risk endangering their lives and those of others.

# THE DARK TRIAD EASILY EXPLAINED

People who have the black triad within them are usually the ones who stand out the most in work environments.

Most of them, are accepted for their great skills they demonstrate on the job.

But on the contrary, they are often opposed by other people for their inability to create personal relationships.

We all have such a person in our work environment.

The boss we hate because he treats us in a rough way, or for other hundred reasons.

But you must know that he does it precisely because he sees that as the only solution to be seen authoritative by the others.

It does not mean that every person in the Dark Triad has all the pathologies described above.

During the rest of this book, we will try to understand in more detail how to behave when a person has maybe only two or even one of the diseases.

We are going to analyze all the possible cases that you can experience in your life where you will find people like that.

But now comes the bigger problem.

Nowadays, we are used to living so-called "toxic" relationships, and we don't realize how much and which people influence us.

The world is a real mess.

This person can be found in your friends or perhaps in your family.

There is only one way to analyze your situation.

You have to break away from everyone momentarily.

You have to look at the situation from afar to understand where the bad apples are.

Take a week to be alone and analyze your surroundings. Carefully examine all the people around you and see what you want to do with them.

If you find that these people do not serve you or that, even worse, use the behaviors of the Dark Triad with you, cut the relationship.

It is not easy to do. You can lose your job if this person is your boss, or you may have to cut off relations with your friend.

But this is what you have to do.

Otherwise, they will take you into the abyss with them.

And I think you don't want that to happen.

Always remember an important fact.
Anyone who has these behaviors does not feel sick.

In most cases, they think the problem it's yours.

They will try to make you feel inferior all the time. But you have to remember one thing.

They're having trouble with their mind, not you.

They are people with an underdeveloped mentality who are not able to keep a minimum of a relationship in any area of their life.

So rest assured and leave them in their beliefs.

# 6 WHAT IS MANIPULATION?

Manipulation is, in short, a form of control that works thanks to changes in the subconscious.

If you have never faced these topics, you will think that the things you are reading are too hard, but stay with me, and you will see that everything will be clearer to you.

As we were saying, manipulation happens between two basic figures, the manipulator and who is going to be manipulated.

All of us, not being aware of it, try to manipulate others.

But we don't have all this control that allows us to decide how to make things happen.

I'll give you a very trivial example. When a baby cries, what is he doing?

Makes a tantrum to manipulate the parent's choice to buy the game, or whatever he craves.

All of us, therefore, try to work on the subconscious of other people with more or less profitable techniques.

## ALL ARE EQUAL

It's not true. Not all people are the same and consequently, they must be treated very differently from each other.

During our life, we will meet an infinity of different and conflicting personalities.

Just think of your co-workers.

There will always be the one you don't like or the one you go out for dinner and drink wine.

Personalities must be read to then modify and manipulate them. You may find the trustful, the selfish, the eternal child, the nice, the cruel, or even the fool.

The key thing is to understand how these people can be controlled.

Better with body language? Or better with the word?

The perfect answer is: it depends.

You have to do a more in-depth analysis of the person in front of you. Before you manipulate you have to analyze.

If you see that the person behaves suspiciously, you will not have an aggressive attitude and vice versa but above all, you must remember what your intent is.

If you want to change his behavior, body language is better. Otherwise, the word will be fine too.

It is critical to understand what dark psychology is and how people who use it manipulate others.

# MANIPULATION OF EMOTIONS

- Now you have discovered what Dark Psychology is in all its details, and you know how to deal with a person who suffers from it if you find it on your way.

- Thanks to this know-how, you should feel relieved and quit.

- You also know that being in front of these people doesn't exactly happen every day.

- Of course, it can happen but it is not something that happens often, fortunately.

- Plus, you are now aware that this thing exists, and you will be able to capture it even before it happens.

- You will stay away from these people without any problem.

- To better understand if a person you meet has this pathology, you need to analyze it in two different ways.

- Both from a clinical and a relational point of view.

- To do this, I will help you with both clinical and relational explanations of every day.

- We will start with the first.

- A clinical theory reveals that the manipulation of emotions only occurs when one person has manipulative behavior.

- That is, the manipulation of emotions is essentially one-sided.

- The relationships that are created from these relationships have three fundamental characteristics:
-  Profiling
- Concealment
- Amorality

In the first case, we find ourselves in a situation where the manipulator has studied the victim's weaknesses.

So he will be able to take advantage of his understanding.

This type of conduct has gotten a lot worse to date.

It happened through the arrival of social networks.

Nowadays, many of the manipulators use this infinity of data that we share with the world to study and understand us.

They know very well what we like and what we don't, and they won't wait long to use them to make us do what they want.

It also happens in work environments.

Often, when someone has all of the employee data at his disposal, such as hours and performance, they will use those to feel more powerful.

So, pay attention to the people you meet.

If a person you've just met or don't know very well seems to know everything about you or what you like or not, watch out.

If I were you, I would be worried. You should investigate the matter and understand how this person knows all this information about you.

But this is the most used method by people with this condition to manipulate you.

In the second case, we find concealment.

This technique allows the manipulator to hide his true intentions behind a friendly behavior but, as we know, this is not the case.

This type of problem occurs mainly in the workplace.
It is unlikely that there is a concealment of behavior in a family or between friends.

The most likely experience in a work environment is that of meeting people who show you to be different compared to what they are.

A person in the workplace can be nice to you, makes jokes, and so on.

But the truth is that these people, in most cases, are ready to stab you in the back as soon as they can.

You have to get out of this situation as soon as possible, especially if you have more power than this person.

They are doing all they can t get to know your weaknesses to understand how to surpass you.

They will be willing to do anything to achieve their goals.

I'm not telling you that all of your colleagues do this but be careful of people's true intentions.
If a person brings you coffee one morning does not mean that he necessarily wants to manipulate you, but maybe he does it only out of kindness.

But if he does it every day and he is not paid for that, be very careful.

A terrible side of these people is that they will try to manipulate you outside the workplace.

That's where they approach you, but that's not where they will act.

It may happen to you at the bar in front of the office. It is common.

They will start asking you favors due to the trust you have already given them, and they will force you to say yes.

A real manipulator will know how to do all this without you even noticing it.

Maybe it has already happened to you, and I'm sorry for you, but now pay more attention to the kind behaviors of people you know little about.

Finally, we find amorality.

When the manipulator has this characteristic he does not know remorse and repentance.

He will have ruthless and treacherous behavior without any kind of problem. No matter how close you are, he won't think about the consequences but will go straight to his goal

One thing you should forget about is the belief that, if you ask this person with courtesy and kindness to stop acting with his behavior, then he would do it.

Even if you have all the reasons in the world and his behavior is neither heaven nor earth, do not do it.

If you do it he will only feel more fulfilled and will target you even more.

If it happens to you at work, that is big trouble.
Most of his actions will not be punished, actually, if you point the problems out, the repercussions will likely be yours.

Many of these people have power. It will be very difficult to assert yourself. Their actions will always be seen as right by others.

Quick example.

If you are an employee of a large company and the boss is rude at you for any reason, it is hard for you to win the fight.

Even if you have all reason on your side.

In this case, get them done and find a way out.

Give him the momentary sop as you prepare to leave.

# 7 CATEGORIES OF BEHAVIOR FOR THE MANIPULATION OF EMOTIONS

Understanding the dynamics that manipulators use to manipulate us is fundamental if we want to avoid them. Many psychologists work on the analysis of these people and, to date, there are countless studies on it.

One of the main features used by the knobs is rewards.

On this subject, the psychologist who first did the studies was Professor Skinner. He put in a cage two mouses, and inside this cage, he placed two levers.

One of these was useless. While the other dropped some food.

In a short time, these animals figured out where to press to eat. This concept is used extensively by emotion manipulators.

Usually, in the form of a compliment or appreciation towards you or something you have done.

But of course, this is not done because he likes you or whatnot. But instead to make you more vulnerable. They do all of this to take your trust and get closer.

It is hard to be ripped off by a person we don't trust, think about it.

We are usually screwed by the very people we trust most. But why does this happen?

Because human beings feel comfortable when they trust others, and for this reason, they stop wondering whether they are doing the right thing or not.

Consequently, the other person is free to do whatever they want. A second behavior that is also used a lot by people in the Dark Triad is negative reinforcement.

A multitude of psychologists have focused on this aspect, but the most interesting experiment has been done by professor Skinner.

Mice have always stayed in cages, but this time, instead of food on the working lever, the psychologist had put an electric discharge that did not kill the animals but only gave them a slight annoyance.

Shortly thereafter, the same animals who previously used the lever to eat stopped pressing it and started with the new lever, which in this case stopped the shaking.

This attitude is found in humans when, for example, you are in a complicated situation like those mice that kept feeling shocks, the manipulator decides to take action and help us.

It takes us out of the trouble momentarily, but he does it to ask for something in return. He won't take no for an answer as he helped you.

The non-stop award.

It is another technique used by manipulators to help control emotions.

I believe that it has happened to all of us to suffer a little.

The intermittent reward technique works very often in love relationships. When a person is dependent on the other, the manipulator gives both positive and negative "rewards" when he wants.

This behavior creates addiction in the other person who goes out of his way to make the partner happy. He fails to understand that he/she is manipulating him for his purposes.

So in a short time, the weakest person will have to submit to everything the other person wants. He will start watching movies and music, for example, that he doesn't like only to please the other person.

And in no time, he will not be able to deal with life in any field due to this evil person who manipulates him.

Another technique used extensively by the most experienced manipulators is punishment.

It is inflicted on the manipulated person if he does not do what the other wants.

This technique can be put into practice by means of screams, yells, and threats, for example.

The most experienced manipulators can make people suffer from these threats, and who is undergoing these abuses does not respond because they are used to it.

It is unfair, and by the time this manner occurs in the manipulated person, the game is over.

Getting out of this crap is hard. You have to have enormous willpower and find that personal pride in us that seems to have been lost.

These cases often result in physical abuse for the person trying to get out. Not sexual abuse, I don't mean that.

But many times, people who have come to be subjected to these levels are physically beaten.

The best thing to do if you find yourself in such a situation is to report everything to a friend or the police.

It won't be an easy choice. Many people, just because they get manipulated, do not understand the seriousness of the situation and think that with time it will improve.

But it will never be better. Indeed, in most cases, not to say always, the situation gets worse. The biggest problem is that the manipulated person thinks the other loves them and doesn't do it out of malice.

Now, if you never found yourself in this situation, it is hard to understand this concept because you will not believe it is possible.

I hope for you that you never get into such a situation. But that's what happens after being manipulated to that point.

# 8 TYPES OF EMOTIONAL MANIPULATION

In addition to all the techniques I mentioned for you in the previous chapter, there are several more subtle manipulations.

Unfortunately, we can encounter these types of manipulation more or less in all our days.

The main techniques are:


- To lie
- Lying 2.0
- To deny
- Rationalize
- Minimize
- Inattention
- Diversion
- Intimidation
- Evasion

These are the main ones we can find, but there would be many others.

In the first position, we find lying.

All people who are part of the Dark Triad and have psychic problems have a strong projection in lying.

The biggest problem is that in most cases, these people are infinitely adept at lying, and, in no time, you will not be able to get back to where the truth is.

Always beware of people who have made you doubt at least once.

Otherwise, they'll screw you before you even know it. Secondly, there is lying 2.0.

I have given this technique such a curious name for a specific reason.

It is the upgrade of the previous technique.
In fact, in this case, the person will not be able to lie shamelessly but will omit fundamental details.

It can happen, for example, if he has to talk about events that have taken place. No one ever knows if it's all or is hiding things.

The main problem is that in most cases, these things are more than fundamental to understand what you are talking about.

Denial is another basic technique for manipulators.

It is used when they have been faced with the fact already happened, but they will not admit their guilt, even in front of evidences.

It, however, has several consequences on the mental level of the manipulator that make him worse and worse in this respect.

It will have happened to you too to find yourself in a similar situation.
Where you have caught a person while committing a crime but he continued to deny making up excuses.

What he's doing is just trying to manipulate you to get away with it.

But, in most cases, when he is in this situation, it never ends well for him.

Let's move on to rationalization.

This technique is used a lot by the big media and marketing pages to pass as good actions that they know very well to be negative.

Similarly, politicians during the rallies say things they know will not be good for the nation, they say them to make people get excited, and for this reason, these words are said without any kind of problem.

In a nutshell, the manipulator explains his abuse but without consequences, because people like those words and they do not understand that this will backfire.
Minimization is very similar to rationalization but with some differences.

In this case, the manipulator makes other people understand well the limits and problems of what he is saying.

But, at the same time, he tends to minimize and reduce the problem to make the person in front of him calm down.

Thus he will be able to limit doubts and will be able to safely achieve his goals.
Now we find the inattention or rather the fake inattention.

In this case, the malicious person decides well at the table the parts of a speech that he will have to deal with.

He does not risk falling into uncomfortable speeches for him but rather precisely creates the whole conversation upstream that will then be held shortly after.

Now let's talk about the diversion.
It is one of the most used techniques in politics today.

It consists of changing the topic when you are in trouble with the question asked.

We see this a little bit in any political interview or debate. People who can manipulate will be able to change the subject very quickly without even making you notice the change.
They will always bring the conversation to their side.

If you want to have fun, go on the internet and look for political meetings and pay attention to the number of times the subject has been changed.

You will be surprised.

After that, there is evasion.

This technique is used by manipulators to make people in front of them convince themselves.

They mainly make comparisons with other people.

For example, this person in the dialogue adds phrases like "as everyone would say" or maybe "other people do this".

He does it basically to ensure that the person who is in front of hearing these words opens his vision and thinks "if others do it too, then it's ok."

This behavior leads the manipulator to use social leverage to get you to do whatever he wants.

Intimidation is another technique used consistently by manipulators.

This technique is expressed by small hidden threats said in a conversation.

We may be in a discussion where the other person or the manipulator makes slight allusions to threats to get us unlocked and tell us what to do.

It mostly happens in work environments in discussions with people who are higher up the corporate hierarchy than you.

From these situations, it is tough to escape unhurt.

The manipulator, in the vast majority of cases, gets the better of us.

# 9 HOW DO I KNOW IF SOMEONE IS MANIPULATING ME?

Are you a reliable, conscious, loyal, and honest person?

I'm sorry for you, but then you are the favorite victim of manipulators.

Manipulators are always looking for this type of people precisely because they are much easier to manipulate and do not find much difficulty.

That is because the manipulative person completely lacks empathy and morality. So he doesn't care in the least to abuse your kindness and good character.

It's just easier for them to attack. By now, these types of people can unfortunately be found in any social class and any environment.

Over the years, manipulators have spread to any field.

We can find it at the top of a multinational company, as well as in every family's father.

Remember, thinking that people are polite with you as a consequence of your kindness is not the smartest idea.

You are not realistic if you think that. You are thinking overly positive. In most cases where you find yourself doing a favor to a person, they will not reciprocate.

In most cases, he will speak badly about you.

That is because the human being is made like this, and even more so are the manipulators.
They will go to great lengths to take any energy you have and then pass it on to another person.

As we have seen above, manipulators use countless techniques to enslave us. This involves a very important fact. Watch out for people you have a lot of trust with.

Most of the time we can indeed find manipulators at work or in any case in those fields, but often we have them at home and we do not notice anything. Within families, there are sometimes great manipulators.

Once, it happened to a great friend of mine.

He had had a family business for several years. He was working in the field of carpentry. His father and uncle worked within the company.

I had always realized from the outside that my uncle was a rather strange person, and I told him so many times. He didn't listen to me. He always replied that they knew each other well and that they were very close so that there would be no problems.

I broke off the conversation by seeing his belief in what he was saying but I wasn't at all sure it was the truth.

One day he writes to me to meet to have a coffee. I knew immediately from his tone that something was wrong and I ran to his house.

Guess what happened?

The uncle had long ago manipulated them to make them open accounts between them and all banking things visible.

One day, his uncle had disappeared along with all the savings of the carpentry shop, $ 200,000 disappeared into thin air.

He heard nothing more about his uncle.

Be aware of all situations that seem safe and trustable to you because those are the most dangerous ones. No expert manipulator stands out while doing it.

Of course, I'm not telling you to be afraid of your family or friends. They are not all manipulators or predators.

However, all the victims of manipulation are unaware of the situation. This is the real problem to be solved.

For this, it is right to know all the techniques of manipulation so we notice once they are used on us.

This way, we will be ready to react in case we realize we are in a manipulative situation.

# 10 PRACTICE MANIPULATIONS EXAMPLES

**Insist on meeting you in a specific place:**

This situation is very often used and sought by the most experienced manipulators.

Both in the workplace and society, it consists of forcing the meeting with the person in a place where the manipulator feels safe while the other person feels lost or otherwise helpless.

This fact happens many times at work. The most classic example is that of the director. Often, the directors of large companies let you into their studio to talk.

They do this for a specific reason. They want you to feel uncomfortable to master the situation and the conversation.
But the same situation is also found in relationships. When you meet for a first date, the other always tries to go to a place where he feels more at ease.

Not everyone does it with the intent to manipulate, but, commonly, it is for that reason.

You will feel in a foreign environment and will be much more vulnerable.

**The premature approach:**

In this case, the manipulator gives you a lot of unwarranted affection and tells you everything intimately. That is done by manipulators when they want to find out about your secrets.

They try to get you intimate right away to make you say something they want to hear.
The work sphere is very afflicted by this practice.

As soon as you maybe learn about something or know things that others ignore, you will see people who have never approached you before that moment, start trying to talk to you as if you were friends for a lifetime.

It has happened to me personally several times.

I used to be the head of a retail company.

You have no idea what the people behind my back were saying, but they behaved well in front of me.

That happens with false people, of course, but also because to manipulate you, they must have a certain closeness with you and try to take it out on these games.

Most people are unable to do it properly, so they get caught in the act, but, if you meet experienced manipulators, I assure you that understanding the situation will be very difficult.

**Always speak first:**

That happens mainly in both long-term relationships but also if you have known each other recently.

When the manipulator enters this phase, he always tries to raise his voice two tones higher than the manipulated person.

All this is done to take control of the conversation and make the other stay silent so that he can decide where the discussion will go.

In most cases, it is the man the manipulator that tries to dominate the one who is the partner in the relationship.

It is a legacy that we have from ancient times where women were subjected to extreme levels, and today this condition no longer exists in most countries but not in all.

To date, this condition of women no longer exists but sometimes, during discussions, the man raises his voice to predominate for this heritage that we have.

It is also true that today in many couples, it is the woman who commands and decides, and the manipulation is done in the opposite direction.

But it is always about manipulation.

**Distortion of the facts:**

If the previous technique was mainly male, the following one is instead more used by the other sex.

Both in work and relationships. Girls always tend to give a distorted view of reality.

You will never know how much a woman paid for a pair of shoes, for example.

When you ask her the price, it is well known that she will reply "in your opinion?"

So you have to guess the price. Anything you say, she will tell you: "are you crazy? It was cheaper than that.

When perhaps she has paid them even more. That is a silly example to disconnect for a moment, but you understand well that this is, in fact, manipulation.

Women are very good at this.

**Bureaucratic bullying:**

Bureaucratic bullying is a present situation in the world of work.

A lot of people have this problem and get manipulated every day.

Now I tell you what it consists of, but first I want to give you an example of the manipulations I undergone, so you will understand what it consists of.

I used to be a bartender. I liked it a lot and when you are a boy you take a lot of money and have fun (in most cases).

I ended up working in a 5-star luxury bar with a world-famous head bartender.

Doing that job became a nightmare. It seemed to be back in a dictatorship. You couldn't talk if he didn't say ok. You could not decide or propose a thing otherwise we were mocked.

I worked 14 hours a day, mentally and physically exhausted.

That is a prime example of bureaucratic bullying.

It happens when a person decides to get under you and will use a million stakes to keep you from doing things and keep you under them.

These people don't care if you are sick or not.

They only see if they can manipulate you or not, and as soon as you do something that doesn't suit them, you are out of the game.

Maybe there will be a bit of resentment in these lines as it is a subject that touches me very personally.

But that's exactly how it is. Stay away from these people if you don't want to live to pay back to them.

Break the chains that keep you stuck in those situations and go back to living for yourself.

These were some of the specific manipulation systems you will come across.

Now we're going to look at all the factors that make you vulnerable to this type of manipulation.

# 11 EVERYTHING THAT MAKES YOU VULNERABLE

To avoid people who would like to manipulate us, we must know what they specifically look for in their victims. A bit like prey, it should understand how to escape the predator without being caught for any reason.

To do this, you need to do a self-analysis job to understand if you have even just one character trait among those that I am going to indicate shortly thereafter.

Many people take it for granted that they are always treated well because it follows the morals and good fellowship that should always be among human beings.

But obviously, this is not the case and it is precisely necessary to understand where we could be attacked.

The biggest problem is that these people hide perfectly among those you don't expect.

They are very good at using the sense of trust that a person has in the world to take advantage of them without restraint.

We have all seen at least one movie where there is a couple which arrives from a foreign city and for whatever reason, they meet a couple of neighbors.

Initially, everything goes well.

They all go out to dinner together, borrow things when they are needed, and so on.

Then when for a futile cause, everything starts to collapse, and a real hate relationship is born between them, and the chaos begins. Fortunately for us, these relationships are not normal but nowadays they have increased more and more.

They can also be found in any social class. None excluded.

Consequently, it has become essential to be aware of these topics to be ready when everything explodes and not be immobile there to suffer situations.

Now to help you understand if you can be another manipulative person, I am going to list a series of specific characteristics that these people look for in their victims.

It doesn't mean that if you are a weak person and you have everything that I will list, you will meet some bad people.

But surely, my dispassionate advice as if we were brothers is to raise your guard.

Always remember that it is wrong, but people take it out on the weakest of them or, rather, those who seem to be less strong.

**The anxiety of being accepted:**

That is a condition that is very easy to find in people today.

This condition has spread even more with the advent of social networks.

Most people's brains are now unbalanced.

The "LIKE" button has changed the lives of millions and millions if not billions of people. Our brain was used to being loaded with dopamine and cortisol from time to time.

Dopamine is released when our brain undergoes a positive impulse, while cortisol is used by our body when a negative thing happens.

These two essences that our body releases make us maintain a certain balance with ourselves.

But to date, the parameters of these have been hit destroyed by social networks. Now everything rounds around that.

When somebody receives likes, his dopamine level rises. Negative comments instead make cortisol levels going up. Three likes and you get dopamine, dopamine, dopamine.

All this due to the complete imbalance of people who are now seeking constant approval from others. Try to weigh it. If you post a photo today and fewer likes arrive, how do you feel?

Maybe you are different and out of these characteristics, but it's hard to believe, and 99% of the time, if you say that you do not have these problems, you are lying to yourself.

You feel sad as if someone had abandoned you.

But nothing serious happened. Indeed, the more detached you are from all these social networks, the better you feel.
For example, I have deleted all of my social accounts.

You don't need them.

Now I'm sure you are thinking about two things. The first is "I could do it but I don't want to because I spend my time there", the second is "it's too excessive, I spend little time a day".

In the vast majority of cases, this is not the case, and if you go on the phone in the settings, it tells you exactly how much time you waste on social networks.

Think that all that time you are being manipulated. You see a world that doesn't exist. On Instagram, guys all have a 6 pack abs, or if you are a girl the others all have fantastic bodies.

Then you go to the beach and ask yourself "but where are the people who are on social media?

Delete them, and you will see how relieved you will feel and will start thinking on your own without being manipulated by anyone.

**The fear of expressing negative emotions:**

Very often, manipulators are overly attracted to people with this trait.

That is all those people who are reluctant to show their negative emotions because they do not want to be misjudged by other people.

The manipulators are just super attracted because they understand that whatever they decide to do to a person with these characteristics, it will be fine, and they will never tell anyone anything.

It happens many times in love relationships.

It is hard to see a manipulator looking for such a person at work. While in relationships it is much more likely that the manipulator is present.

**The inability to say no:**

People with this trait always think that saying no is wrong if you do that, then you are not a nice person, and they want to be so.

The main problem is that you should look at your interests first and then those of others. Also because, if a person asks you something, he is thinking of himself. Try to think about it.

But manipulators are super adept at making the person think they have to stay under and have to follow everything the other says.

That often happens in the workplace.

Where there is the boss who decides, everyone obeys and no one can say no. In that case, you are undergoing a manipulation that will cause you to remain a slave to that person in the long run.

It will initially ask you to do this and do that. It starts with small favors until he gets to control you as if he had a magic wand.

**Little self-sufficiency:**

It is precisely the icing on the cake that manipulators are looking for. When people are looking for help of any kind, they risk running into a manipulator who will be ready to take advantage of this.

That is because once the manipulator has helped you, the favor that he will ask you will be ten times greater.

You must avoid this situation like death. When you need a hand, only go to people who you are sure will help you with nothing in exchange, or who will not do it again in the future.

**Absence of self-direction:**

It is very similar to the previous one but has some essential differences. It is not about helping someone who has a problem. Here the person is lost.

Not in the sense that he has to go to a club and doesn't know which way to take, but he can't understand what he wants from life or what to do in a particular situation in his life.

Here all the possible manipulators that you can meet come out. I see a great opportunity. A person who has no idea what to do is the best thing that can happen to a manipulator.

He brings him to do what he wants. It will lead him to make choices just because he manipulated him well.

People in this situation are alike the holy grail of manipulators.

**Genuineness:**

Perhaps one of the worst conditions is genuineness.

This condition is greatly exploited by the manipulators of the sale. They use people's ingenuity to rip them off and steal their money.

This condition is not always visible in the person, but it often comes out in times of difficulty. Many victims of manipulators are precisely people in economic difficulties.

When a manipulator sees that a person is in trouble with money, he uses the latter's feelings to make him trust the manipulator who offers him quick and easy money.

It is a highly incorrect policy that manipulative people adopt on temporarily weak people.

I'll give you an example of a weak person momentarily to make it clearer to you.

If someone finds himself in the situation of having to send his child to a college but does not have the money for it, he may find someone, online or in presence, it makes no difference, that guarantees him to find the money just by clicking here and there on your computer.

**What do you think the person does?**

It doesn't mean being stupid, and most of the time, people who fall for these tricks know very well that you don't get rich that easily.

But the skilled manipulator succeeds with a series of sentences that destroy all the security of the manipulated person, and, in a short time, brings him to his side.

This technique is unfair because it plays on the feelings of the people and most of the time the manipulator takes everything that the person has and destroys his life.

Manipulators succeed easily, without even putting in too much effort.

**No self-esteem:**

These people are always highly sought after by manipulators for one simple reason. With a few compliments and a few nice words, they manage without any problem to bring the victim to their side.

Unfortunately, many people have this problem nowadays. The increase in this phenomenon has amplified by the fact that people seek attention on the internet.

That creates anxiety and a sense of inadequacy, and the manipulators feed on this situation.

**Submissive personality:**

People who believe in others don't have to be ashamed or anything like that, but they need to know that they are among the most coveted prey of manipulators.

Many of them approach the person to make them start to think well of them. But after gaining the trust of the person, the manipulator can easily play his game.

**Immaturity:**

It is another feature highly sought after by manipulators.

Immature people are overly malleable and this makes them one of the most desired people.

This is what happens to all those kids who are manipulated by groups to become part of them. But this leads kids on the wrong track and make them slaves of these people.

Just a few can get out of the loop because most of the people will feel addicted to it and this will tie them to the manipulators. The latter will lead them more and more on the bad road for their convenience.

How many guys have you seen changing in a short time just because of their new friends?

I imagine many, as I have seen. Of course, friendships change for a million reasons ranging from fights to moving to another country.

But the most important thing is to understand who you are approaching and see if these people are the ones we want to date without the fear of being alone.

## Impressionability:

Manipulators looking for this character can be easily found on the internet. Social networks are full of these people.

People who flaunt things they don't have or show a false lifestyle only to get the attention of impressionable people so that they can be manipulated with ease.

They do it mainly to sell something to these people and take away the money for a product or service that the person buys to become like the manipulator.

Of course, none of these methods ultimately work and so in a short time, all will have been in vain.

**Narcissism:**

It is an unexpected feature, doesn't it? I already see you saying: but how is that possible? Manipulators are narcissists, so how could they go after narcissists like them?

Well, they do. And for a simple reason.

As I explained to you earlier, Narcissists always want to be in the center of attention, and manipulators know this well and use it in their favor. They start to compliment them so that they can get them on their side, and they will take the trust of these people.

**Impulsiveness:**

Impulsiveness increases the chances of being manipulated.

That happens for a reason. When a person is impulsive, he does not pay attention to the consequences of his actions, and, for the manipulators, this is the icing on the cake.

They play a lot with this aspect of people because with a minimum of effort they can make the victim do what they want.

Sometimes they manifest this by causing them to explode. They harm the victim or tell him words that they know affect that person because at that moment they maybe want them to go crazy

Or maybe they do the opposite.

They calm the victim and make them feel good because they may know that this will bring many benefits to them.

**Materialism:**

Unfortunately, this is a deeply rooted part of modern society.

Where people are placed in classes based on their material possessions and our whole life is now destined to run after objects of which we could live without.

Manipulators use this aspect to their advantage.

They give materials and objects to their victims so they will be happy and grateful to this person and will begin to follow him in everything they do without objecting a single time.

**Be very careful of all those people who seem so nice to you even if they know little about you because they are just trying to buy your trust.**

# Final words

Improving your observation skills might be an easier task than you would think. You most likely are already interpreting body language every day without realizing it. Think about the friendliest employee you encounter in your workplace. Do they smile when you pass them in the hall? Do they maintain eye contact and nod when you talk to them? Their body language likely contributes to your perceiving them as friendly.